The Creatures Of Chichester
The one about the golden lake.

Christopher Joyce

DEDICATION
For Zoe and Fin

With thanks to Eric, Gerry and Jan for their editing skills and Mariia Kudrina for her amazing illustrations.

Published by
Chichester Publishing
Copyright © 2017 Christopher Joyce.

Cover design Jane Dixon-Smith

All rights reserved.

ISBN: 978-0-9935814-5-8

Introduction by Jacqui Flisher –
Dip.RSA – DTTLS - Dyslexia Specialist and Educationalist
A New Way Education Limited - West Berkshire. www.a-new-way.co.uk

I was delighted when Christopher asked me to pen a few words as an Introduction to his latest book in the 'Creatures of Chichester' series, especially when he revealed that one of the main characters – Jacob – is dyslexic.
This book is of course a work of fiction. What Christopher has so succinctly managed to do, is to capture not only the real life issues faced by many dyslexic individuals but also to highlight the unique problem solving, creative, out of the box thinking skills which are the essence of the dyslexic way of thinking, learning and perceiving the world. So perhaps this book would be best described as a work of fiction and fact.
Over the years, I have worked with

and helped many thousands of dyslexic individuals, so I can relate to the very real sense of frustration and anger that not only Jacob, but many struggling readers often experience and the effect this can have on their confidence and self-esteem.

Views on dyslexia are thankfully changing, albeit very slowly, but there is light at the end of the tunnel and dyslexia is becoming more recognised for what it really is, not a learning disability, but the unique ability to be able to think, learn and view things in a different way.

As you progress through the story, it becomes increasingly clear that Jacob's ability to see things differently, not only saves Chichester but ultimately the world.

In reality, the world is going to need more 'Jacob's' in order for our planet to progress, become a better place for us all but just like in the story, to ultimately survive.

CONTENTS

1 Happy New Year — 01
2 The Music Fades Away — 11
3 Beaky Spreads The Word — 21
4 Chilling Times — 31
5 Rumblings From Below — 40
6 The Golden Lake — 50
7 Secrets At Edes House — 60
8 Trapped In The Attic — 69
9 Magic Mirrors — 79
10 Dastardly Plans Revealed — 89
11 Superfish To The Rescue — 97
12 Animal Army Attack — 108

1 HAPPY NEW YEAR.

The golden waters that flooded the city and the snowstorm that followed were just the beginning, but the Twolegs of Chichester will never know how close it was to the end.

Jacob was playing the piano in his bedroom. He had been allowed to stay up late – it was New Year's Eve, after all. He'd escaped the shouting and silly games played by the adults downstairs for the security of his beloved piano. The grown-ups called him a musical genius but also whispered that they were worried about him not being able to read very well.

It was true that the words and letters got all muddled up when he tried to read, which made him angry sometimes, so he'd spend twenty minutes bashing away at the piano until the music just carried him away. But tonight, at the stroke of midnight, the music mysteriously carried on by itself long after he lifted his fingers from the keyboard.

At first, the adults couldn't hear it. They were too busy hugging and kissing each other to welcome in the New Year. Jacob could hear it though; he went to the window to look out into the night. He could see other children staring through their curtains as well.

The music seemed to be coming from the trees that looked like black skeletons in the glare of the lamplight. It was like the sound of a bass guitar playing low notes to gently push the melody along.

Jacob was quite tall for ten, so most people thought he was older. He put on his thick winter coat, tucked his unruly red hair into a warm woolly hat, slipped downstairs, and stepped out through the front door. His breath made wispy grey trails in the icy air; he pulled up the collar of his coat and shoved his hands into his pockets.

The music was a little louder now, and as he brushed past the grasses by the garden gate, he noticed that they were making soft ringing noises as they touched the hem of his coat.

Other Twolegs were now coming out into the street and staring at the grass that had picked up the beat of the music. Some of the adults were swaying back and forth and dancing in little circles. The shrubs and flowers were not to be left out and made trumpeting sounds that slid in perfectly to the melody.

Jacob touched the majestic birch tree standing just yards from his house and felt a warm vibration flow through his body. It was like the rush of excitement you get when you first learn to ride a bike but deeper and longer lasting. A huge grin filled his face and he reached out his hand to his dad, who had followed with the others out of the party.

'What's going on, Dad?'

'I'm not sure, but it's really amazing. Can you feel it?'

'It's like a million butterflies bursting into the light. I love it. If only Mum could be here.'

Jacob's dad held him tight and wiped away a tear. Milly had been gone a few years now, but they still thought of her every day. She had been ill for just a few months before she'd said her final farewell.

Jacob still thought it was unfair and sometimes shouted at the walls in frustration. When that happened, his friends didn't know what to say. Sorry seemed a bit rubbish, so they usually just said nothing. Jacob would sit by his garden pond and talk to the goldfish instead.

He loved the fish in the pond

– his mum had named them all.

There was Zorro that had a black Z on his head, and Fantail, who seemed very proud of her long billowing tail. Ghost and Silver were white in colour, while in contrast, Sharky was almost pure black. But his favourite of them all was Dr Carrasius Hope.

He was a glowing gold colour that lit up the water when he swam past the pond lights at night. Jacob's mum thought up the name after she'd been at St Richard's Hospital for a few weeks.

It was one of the days when she was feeling well, so they'd gone to the garden centre, which also sold big plastic ponds and, most importantly, hundreds of different kinds of fish.

Jacob would nag his parents to go there and imagined himself swimming in the warm water with the beautiful tropical fish. He loved to walk among the tanks and run his fingers over the labels containing weird and wonderful names written in a strange language.

His mum explained that this was Latin and it was used all over the world so that no matter where you lived or what language you usually spoke, there was always one name for each fish that remained the same.

She even tried to get him to spell out Car-ras-ius, which was the Latin name for a goldfish. That was when she decided to call their new goldfish Dr Carrasius Hope. Jacob just called him Doc, which used to make his mother laugh.

Even those Twolegs that had been watching TV were now hugging the trees and recording the music on their phones. Nobody seemed scared. It was impossible not to smile as the tunes became brighter and more complex and the lovely vibrations filled everyone's bodies.

'Is this really happening?' Jacob whispered to his dad as he stroked the dry papery bark of the birch tree.

'Well, I'm not sure if we're on some sort of prank TV show. I can't see any cameras, but it is stunning, isn't it?' He wrapped both his arms around his son and they swayed to the music.

Nobody had noticed that their pets could also hear the music. Rabbits pushed their quivering noses against the wire of their hutches, puppies and kittens woke from their dreams of warmth and milk, and even the fish in the garden pond paused to listen.

But the creatures could hear more than just the music. They also heard bone-chilling whispers and cold laughter and knew that they had to stop the music before it was too late.

2 THE MUSIC FADES AWAY.

The next morning was New Year's Day. It was to be a year that everyone in Chichester would remember. The city was surrounded by ancient stone walls that were as tall as a house in some places. Over many hundreds of years, some of the stones had been removed to build new houses, or broken up to allow roads into the city. They were like the edge of a crusty pizza. And right in the middle of the 'pizza' was a large stone cross, where the Twolegs of Chichester would gather to chat and meet up with friends.

The Cross was more like a big umbrella, which sheltered everyone from the snow and rain. It had large arches decorated with stone animals whose faces had washed away over the years. Four clocks faced down each of the main streets leading from the Cross to the city walls.

North Street was full of stylish shops and trendy restaurants that led to the theatre. South Street, which was also packed with fashionable shops and coffee houses, led down to the railway station. West Street was home to the majestic cathedral that dominated the city centre, and East Street had yet more shops and places to eat and drink, leading out towards the green fields and countryside beyond.

Jacob lived just off East Street in a large house near the art gallery. His dad was a doctor at the hospital and his mum had been a teacher in the posh private school next door to the cathedral.

The school was also hundreds of years old. Many of the pupils sang every day at the cathedral and nearly all of them could play the piano, guitar, trumpet, or indeed anything that made a tune. His mum had taught music and Jacob wondered whether she could hear the music that played everywhere last night.

Jacob went to a smaller school in the centre of town. It was just a short walk from the cathedral and only a few pupils at his school liked to play music. His best friend, Ethan, played guitar, just a few chords really, but he said that one day they would be in a boy band and tour the world. Ethan put product in his hair to make it stand on end and always wore cool T-shirts. If he took off his glasses, he could almost get away with the boy-band look.

Ethan had also stayed up late to celebrate the New Year and the next morning had rushed around to Jacob's house and banged on the front door.

'It's open,' shouted Jacob's dad from the kitchen.

Ethan burst through the door and disappeared in a blur as he dashed up the stairs to Jacob's room.

'Hi, Ethan,' Mr Buckley said to empty space as he walked over

and closed the open door.
'Happy New Year to you too.'

The boys excitedly shared their stories of the night before. Ethan said that the TV crews had already arrived. They could hear the buzz of helicopters above. They flicked on the TV in Jacob's room and saw a man they recognised from one of the news channels interviewing the mayor of Chichester at the Cross.

The mayor wore his gold chains of office with great pride as if he'd invented the music himself. He puffed out his chest and said, 'We are still investigating where the music came from and if there is any danger to the people that heard it. It faded away after twenty minutes or so, and we have our esteemed professors from the university looking into it.'

A group of educated-looking men and women nodded wisely behind the mayor. They all wore glasses that wiggled on their noses, reflecting the light of the cameras. Some carried clipboards and others some sort of radiation counters. In Jacob's opinion, they looked as if they had absolutely no idea where the music had come from but were never going to admit that.

The TV reporter then played a video that someone had taken on their iPhone. It was a bit blurred and dark, but you could see everyone hugging the trees and swaying to the music.

'Do you think it was aliens trying to contact us?' asked Ethan.

'No, it didn't feel like it was coming from space to me. You could almost smell it. It faded away after the fireworks ended. It didn't sound like happy music to me, more kind of threatening.'

The boys texted a few friends and decided to investigate more. Jacob's dad told them to be back for lunch as they shot past him in the kitchen.

'And don't slam the ... never mind.' He was glad to see Jacob having fun and sat down to watch the news with a hot cup of tea.

The spiders of North Street had also heard the music. Button and his sister, Stitchley, had lived at the store in North Street for longer than anyone could remember. It had been a smart menswear shop when they first moved in.

Then it became a bridal shop; now it was a charity shop to support the local hospice. The spiders were well liked by the other creatures in town and quite famous for solving many mysteries over the years.

They'd found Streak the missing puppy, solved the mystery of a terrible fire in South Street, and even helped find missing children after they disappeared in the horrendous storms that had raged over the city. Button was excited that this could be the start of a new adventure.

'It's all been a little dull of late. Shall we meet with the other creatures in town and see if we can find out what's going on?' asked Button.

His sister crawled down from her web and looked him straight in one of his eight eyes. She was quite a bit bigger than him, and for a moment she looked like she might eat him.

'You really can't sit still for a moment, can you?' She loved her brother and had to admit that the singing plants were truly amazing, even if she was slightly troubled by the whispers in the background of the song.

'Why don't we get everyone together this evening? We'll meet at the Cross at midnight. The camera crews and Twolegs should have drifted away by then. I'll tell the pigeons on the roof to spread the word. They're such gossips that everyone will know by lunchtime.'

Christopher Joyce

3 BEAKY SPREADS THE WORD.

Stitchley crept up onto the roof of the shop and spinked to Beaky, a pigeon with little brain and dirty grey feathers. She regularly perched on the roof to catch the warmth from the winter sun.

Like most of the animals in Chichester, they could spink to each other. This was like speaking your thoughts. It was strictly against the rules to even think of eating another creature when they spinked to you – and besides – Beaky liked chips and burgers more than spiders.

'Beaky, can you spread the word that Button and I are having a meeting at the Cross this evening to discuss the singing plants?'

'Who said dat?' spinked the startled pigeon in reply.

'It's Stitchley the spider, Beaky. I'm down by the gutter.'

Beaky squinted in the morning sun and spotted Stitchley waving her legs at her.

'You look like you is dancing to da music from last night. It was freaky, wan'it?'

'Yes, Beaky, we think the Twolegs may need our help.'

'OK. I'll get the gang to spread the word. See you at midday at the museum.'

'Midnight at the Cross!'

spinked Stitchley as loudly as she could.

'Oh yeah. Dat's what I meant.'

Beaky flew off and Stitchley returned to the warmth of the shop, hoping for the best.

Jacob, Ethan, and their friend Zoe were sitting on a bench by the pond in Jacob's garden. Zoe was in the same class as the boys and rugby mad. She never wore dresses and could whistle louder than anyone in town. Her long blond hair was tucked under a warm bobble hat.

Ethan was dead clever and always came top in English and maths. He tried to help Jacob with his reading and sometimes would let him peep over his shoulder in spelling tests. That was until their teacher, Miss Cobblestone, had caught them.

The other kids would sometimes hide Ethan's glasses until Zoe would pin one of the bullies against the wall and force him to return them.

Zoe was peering into the water. The fish were supposed to be hibernating at the bottom of the pond at this time of year, but were all quite close to the surface.

'Should we feed them?'
'I don't think you're supposed to in the winter,' replied Ethan. 'They're supposed to be sleeping.'

'That's my point,' said Zoe. 'How would you feel if you woke up from a long nap 'cos some nutter was playing a trumpet in your ear and you couldn't find anything to eat?'

'Let's see if they're still lively tomorrow. Maybe we could give them a bit of food then,' said Jacob.

Zoe was not impressed and dug into the pocket of her duffle coat for some old mints and bunged a few in her mouth as if to make the point.

Doc and the other goldfish were indeed quite lively. The waves of music had travelled clearly through their pond and they'd heard the whispers too. Doc was very frustrated that he could not go to the meeting at the Cross later that night. He'd overheard a robin tell one of the blackbirds that the spiders had called everyone together.

'They never ask us. It's so unfair,' he said to Sharky, who was swimming nearby.

'Well, it's not exactly as if we could do much down at the Cross other than flap our tails and gasp for breath,' he replied.

'That's not the point,' said Doc, leaping out of the pond in anger. 'Just because we're under water doesn't mean we're stupid. I have a brain, you know. Nobody ever thinks of us down here.'

The school friends heard a faint plop as Doc fell back into the pond.

'He looks hungry to me,' said Zoe, sucking on her mints.

'Let's go up to the university,' said Ethan. 'I heard that they're having a news conference at lunchtime today.'

'Okay, but I'll have to text my dad to tell him I'll be late for lunch. I'll do it now.'

Jacob's dad got the text just as he was putting some pies in the oven. With a sigh, he took them back out and returned them to the fridge. He was mildly annoyed at having to change his lunch plans, but it was good to see Jacob out of the house and away from his keyboard for a change.

They could always have a late lunch after the news conference. He had to be back at the hospital tomorrow – all this fuss about musical plants would have to wait. His diary was full and his patients always came first.

The boys and Zoe walked along East Street and then along New Park Road to the university. It wasn't a big university. Most of the students studied music and theatre or sports subjects. It was just next to St Richard's Hospital and Jacob often heard the students cheering for their football or rugby teams as he waited for his dad to finish work.

They arrived at the university as everyone was piling into the Showroom, a large theatre space where the dance and drama students would perform. It held about two hundred people, and today it was standing room only. Jacob and the others crept up the side stairs to the back of the room.

The camera crews and journalists were jostling for the best position, and one of them shoved Zoe aside to get a better view. She was considering shoving her back when suddenly the lights in the theatre dimmed and a spotlight lit up a speaker's lectern on the stage.

Professor MacKrell took to the stage and waved his hands to quieten the audience. He was so thin that he looked like he might blow over in a strong wind. He slid his glasses down his large curved nose and glared at a few reporters in the front row who were still talking. Under his fierce stare, the room fell silent.

Three more bespectacled professors crept in at the back of the stage and took their seats. Zoe nudged Ethan in the ribs and whispered, 'It looks like trout face at the back could do with a good suntan.' The pale-faced lecturer stared out into the dark as if she'd heard Zoe's comment, then turned her attention back to Professor MacKrell.

'I have some grave news,' announced the professor. Then all the lights went out.

Christopher Joyce

4 CHILLING TIMES.

The theatre was pitched into total darkness until someone managed to stagger blindly to the door and push it open. Weak winter light crept into the room and a few of the media people waved their phones around to create little arcs of brightness in the dark.

There was a buzzing noise, like a wasp trapped in a jam jar, and the lights flickered back into life. A shocked gasp filled the room as everyone stared at the professors on the stage. They had turned to ice.

Professor MacKrell had a rather startled expression on his face; a large icicle hung off his hooked nose. Like the other lecturers behind him, he was frozen in position as if playing statues. One hand held out his icy spectacles; the other was curled up in a fist on the lectern. His skin shimmered in the glaring stage lights as if scattered with glitter.

A man with a large microphone slowly approached the icy figure and prodded Professor MacKrell. 'He's absolutely solid,' he whispered to himself as much as to the gawping crowd.

The silence was shattered as dozens of reporters fought their way to the stage to take pictures. Punches were thrown and hair pulled as they battled their way to the front rows of the theatre.

Jacob, Ethan, and Zoe were bundled aside, although Zoe did manage to trip up the reporter that had earlier shoved her hard in the ribs. The three friends stood on the chairs to get a better look. But all they could see was Professor MacKrell's frozen body surrounded by a hungry pack of journalists with cameras flashing away like crazy.

More reporters rushed up to the other professors on stage, who were also frozen. The angry reporter that Zoe had tripped up a few moments earlier pushed her way to the front and fell against one of the icy bodies. It toppled to the floor and shattered into a thousand pieces as it hit the floor.

Everyone stopped to stare at the shards of ice scattered on the floor. Zoe and Ethan were amazed to see that Jacob had crawled through the throng of people to reach the stage. He grabbed the microphone that Professor MacKrell had been using and shouted, 'Everyone stand still!'

Ethan was speechless, as he'd never seen his friend take control like this before.

Jacob continued. 'We have to get the remaining professors into a freezer before any more damage is done. The university kitchens are just opposite. Everyone gently lift the frozen bodies. Try not to break off anything and, for goodness' sake, put down your cameras.

These people need our help!'

A few more cameras flashed as everyone started to carefully pass the frozen torsos towards the open doors. Zoe and Ethan were ahead of the crowd and rushed into the kitchen to the large walk-in freezer stocked with lamb, beef, pork, and dozens of other frozen foods to feed the hungry students.

They threw out the icy produce and slid out the shelves. There was just enough room to get Professor MacKrell and the other two lecturers into the freezer. Jacob slammed the door shut as more cameras flashed in his face.

Pesto watched on from a shelf high up in the kitchen. The intrepid mouse had recently moved into the university with his girlfriend, Laplancha. They had decided to move out of the Italian restaurant in East Street, as it was getting too crowded and they risked getting stepped on. Laplancha had said that as the students were away for most of the summer and for long periods over Christmas, it would be more peaceful. Not today it wasn't!

Pesto was quite a handsome mouse with silky white fur and perfect little pink ears. He adored Laplancha's eyes that shone like black diamonds in the light created by the cameras. They reflected the chaos below as she huddled beside him.

'Nice and peaceful,' whispered Pesto. 'Leave the crowds behind. It will be lovely.'

'Shush,' said Laplancha. 'It was

until today, but this is madness. I heard that the spiders have called for a meeting at the Cross tonight, but this can't wait. Come on, let's get out of here and go see them.'

Her cream-coloured fur was fluffed up to its warmest as she poked her nose outside the kitchen door. Pesto was right behind her as they made a dash across the frost-covered playing fields to the hedges that ran down to the busy road.

They stopped for a moment to catch their breath and then scampered along through the fallen leaves until they reached College Lane.

Pesto could hear sirens as ambulances and police cars raced to the university; the helicopters buzzed above them as news crews arrived to cover the breaking story. The noise was deafening as they dashed across the road and into Priory Park. Gasping for breath, they hid amongst the roots of an old oak tree. The spiders lived just the other side of the park. A short walk for Twolegs but quite a distance for two small mice.

They were about to set off again when they heard a soft humming noise that seemed to come from the roots of the tree. It sounded like violins playing a sad song in the distance. Then they heard the evil cackling in the background of the song and knew they had no time to lose.

5 RUMBLINGS FROM BELOW.

Jacob's dad was glued to the TV. His phone had been beeping like crazy as friends and family texted him to say his son was on the news. And sure enough, there was a replay of Jacob and his friends carrying the frozen bodies into a freezer and slamming the door. TV vans had pulled up outside his house; there were already a dozen or so reporters shouting for an interview when Jacob and his pals snuck in the back door.

'It's gone crazy out there,' said Zoe. 'We had to tunnel our way through the mob to get out of the university.'

Jacob's dad hugged his son tight. 'Are you okay? That must have been very scary. I'm proud of you for taking control. Good lad.'

Jacob was still breathing heavily after the dash from the university. He took a moment to rest his head on his dad's arm.

'I'm okay. But one of those professors is in little pieces all over the stage and the others are not looking too good. What's going on, Dad?'

'I don't know, but let's get you three something to eat. You must be starving. Oh, and don't answer the phone or open the door to anyone. We need time to think.'

The mice, Pesto and Laplancha, reached the charity shop in North Street at about the same time as Jacob arrived home. They scampered through the open door when someone left the shop with a big bag of old books and CDs. Button and Stitchley were nowhere to be seen. Then they heard a small voice spink to them from under a bookcase in the corner.

'We're over here,' spinked Button. 'Tell us what you've seen.'

The mice updated the spiders about the frozen professors and resting in Priory Park, where they'd heard the song drifting up from the roots of the tree.

'Beaky has done a good job,' spinked Stitchley, stretching her eight furry legs. 'That pigeon is not as dumb as she looks.

There should be a large gathering at the Cross tonight. Hopefully all the attention will have moved to the university, so we should be able to meet in peace.'

*

The four clocks at the top of the Cross lit up the empty streets. Most of the Twolegs were glued to their television screens or locked safely in their homes. Police cars had toured the city, asking everyone to remain calm and stay indoors. The helicopters hovered over the university to the north of the city. Button observed the gathered throng.

He'd never seen so many creatures in one place before. He recognised Knuckles and Streak, the brave dogs from Penfold's butchers'. They had gathered together twenty or more pooches of all shapes and sizes. They were hunkered down out of the winter breeze next to the shoe shop at the top of South Street.

Plectrum, the rabbit from the music shop in East Street, headed up a collection of bunnies, gerbils, and hamsters keen to help. Stitchley pointed out the golden fur of Shandy, the hamster from the pub in South Street.

The small rodents kept their distance from the pride of cats and kittens led by Purrcasso, the beautiful Bengal cat from the art gallery.

A flock of birds, headed up by the budgies Sparkle and Topaz, were perched on the turrets of the Cross. It was, without doubt, the biggest gathering any of them could remember.

The hands on all four of the clocks jolted into the vertical position just as Button slid down on a silken thread to address the crowd.

'Thank you all for coming and trusting each other in these difficult times. You've all heard the music. Most of you will also know about the icy goings-on at the university today. We don't know if they are linked, but we assume they might be. Have any of you any ideas where this is all coming from?'

There was a muttering amongst the creatures and then Codger, the old mole from the hospice, raised his large paws and spinked, 'The sound of silence is as loud as thunder. Music makes you dance from a place down under.'

A hushed silence fell over the creatures as they tried to understand what they had heard. Codger had lived in the city longer than anyone else, and he often spoke in riddles. The younger creatures would get a clip on the ear for mocking him. Their parents knew he always had something important to say.

Beaky fluttered down from one of the golden flags that adorned the top of the Cross. 'Yeah, dat's a really good point. I hate thunder.'

The mole nodded wisely and Beaky pecked at a bit of chewing gum stuck under the central seat of the cross.

'I'm sorry,' spinked Stitchley from her web next to Button. 'Codger, can you explain a little more?'

All the creatures leaned forward. Everyone was focused on the small greying mole with his tiny black eyes blinking in the street lights.

'Rocket man. Walking in a winter wonderland,' spinked the mole as he shook his head, a little confused.

'He's just remembering old songs from years ago,' whispered one of the cats. 'I think he's lost the plot.' A few of the dogs growled at this rudeness and the cat slid back into the shadows.

'Yellow river, yellow river,' hummed Codger to himself as if lost in a memory from long ago.

Some of the animals shook their heads in sadness. It really did look like their brave old friend was very confused. Then a shout went up from Pesto. The mouse had one of his tiny pink ears placed on the pavement near the Cross. 'Listen! It's the sound of running water!'

Cats, dogs, hamsters, and rabbits all placed their ears to the ground as they heard the gurgling and churning of water coming from the earth at their feet.

'The canal at the bottom of South Street has burst its banks,' spinked a panicked seagull from the top of the Cross. 'There's a flood coming. Get to safety, everyone!'

The Creatures of Chichester

6 THE GOLDEN LAKE.

By noon of the following day, the water was everywhere. Doc, the goldfish, and his friends watched in amazement as their little pond merged with the other streams of water to form a restless lake that covered the city. The oddest thing was that the water seemed to stop at the city walls. It rose as if it were being held back by invisible glass until it was at least three feet deep.

Most of the Twolegs had no

idea about the flood until they came downstairs to find their kitchen stools and tables bobbing around in the water. The strangest thing of all was that this water was not brown and stinking of sewage; it smelled of daffodils and was a bright golden colour.

The yellow river seemed to flow in a clockwise direction around the Cross. Small waves lapped against the seat of the old monument, which had been packed with all sorts of creatures just a few hours ago.

When Button realised what was happening, he'd quickly instructed the gathered animals to check that the other creatures in the city were OK. Dogs searched the gardens for any hutches that needed to be moved to safety and pawed at the doors to free any trapped animals. Birds flew to all corners of the city to alert any moles and other burrowing creatures to get to higher ground.

Cats and mice searched for any insects asleep in the long grass and spinked that they had to crawl higher. Everyone played their part so that none of the creatures were lost.

The Twolegs were also safe, if a bit soggy, as nearly all of them slept upstairs in their homes. They now peered out through the windows of their houses at the shimmering yellow waters as rescuers helped some of the older Twolegs into boats.

Helicopters buzzed overhead, unaware that Doc and pond creatures from all over the city had gathered at the Cross.

There were goldfish and sticklebacks, several beautiful koi carp with orange and white patches, and even a few frogs and toads. They had all heard the whispers and were drawn to the centre of town.

Doc spinked to the others. 'So the yellow river has come to Chichester and for once we are free to swim wherever we like. But be careful; it won't be long before the Twolegs get out their nets and fishing rods, so be wary of worms on hooks. It's our time to save the city.'

'Save the city from what?' spinked a scared stickleback next to him. 'I liked my pond just as it was. It's scary out here.' Quite a few of the other fish swished their tails in agreement.

Doc wasn't afraid. He'd longed

all his life to escape the confines of his little pond. He'd heard about a huge wide world out there that he could never see. Dragonflies had told tales about flowing rivers and canals full of fish. They'd shared songs about the land-based creatures living alongside the Twolegs and described how other animals were free to roam the fields. Doc had listened to these stories all his life and dreamed of swimming in a huge shoal of fish to the ends of the Earth. Now was his chance.

*

Jacob had always loved the water. He had a two-seater canoe that he'd built with his dad when he was only six years old. They'd made a frame of wood and then stretched thick canvas over the frame and covered it with a type of glue to make it watertight. Jacob had helped paint it a bright red. He'd loved it ever since. As soon as the waters had started to rise, his dad had fetched the canoe from the shed at the bottom of the garden. It was now tied up alongside his kitchen door.

Jacob's dad had been on the phone most of the morning to his team at the hospital. St Richards was outside the city walls and had escaped the flood. They still had power and hundreds of townsfolk had turned up with injuries where they'd slipped or fallen over in their panic to get out of the water. He was needed at the hospital and reluctantly agreed that Jacob could paddle him to the edge of the golden lake so he could help the injured.

'After you drop me off, go straight home. Do you hear?'

Jacob agreed, but the sheer joy of paddling around the city overwhelmed him, and just a few minutes later he'd already met up with Ethan and their friend Zoe.

Ethan lived in a new house on the banks of the canal. It was not far from the police station at the far end of South Street. He also loved the water and had a small wooden canoe that was stored in the roof space of his garage. He'd managed to get to it before the water rose too high and had collected Zoe, who was now beaming from ear to ear.

They'd agreed to meet near the cathedral and paddled

along West Street. They gawped at the water lapping up against the doors of parked cars half-submerged in the golden water. It was scary but also very exciting to be gliding along the streets they knew so well. They reached the gates of the posh school, where musical instruments of all sorts were being handed out of the windows to be taken to safety.

Some of the teaching staff had managed to get their hands on an old speedboat. A cello was handed down to a man in the boat, which wobbled dangerously from side to side. A huge cry went up as the boat toppled to one side and teachers, pupils, and instruments were all thrown into the water.

Fortunately, it was still only a

few feet deep, so after an initial panic, most of them found their feet and splashed around, trying to stop the cello and guitars from floating down the street. That was when Jacob noticed that it was harder to paddle his canoe and saw the ice begin to spread out across the lake.

The Creatures of Chichester

7 SECRETS AT EDES HOUSE.

Ice crystals formed in Jacob's nose as the temperature dropped. He paddled as fast as he could to help the last few pupils struggling to get out of the water; his breath was visible as puffs of white water vapour. Zoe and Ethan were yelling at everyone to get to dry land.

    Snow started to swirl around the spire of the cathedral. Within minutes it became a blizzard of white flakes that danced and glistened in the

winter's afternoon light.
Everyone was scrambling to get out of the water. Some of the children were already wrapped in blankets taken from the school dormitory.

Jacob and his friends paddled through the icy water to the steps of a grand old house opposite the cathedral. They leapt out of the canoes and hurried inside, where they found themselves in a very elegant entrance with cream panelled walls that were decorated with old paintings in golden frames.

Above the wooden panels, gold-coloured wallpaper reflected the light from a huge chandelier that hung in front of a marble fireplace. Jacob had visited the house on a school trip last term and tried to recall when it was built.

'It's Georgian of course,' said Ethan, observing Jacob's puzzled frown. 'It's called Edes House. Don't you remember? We came here when we were studying the history of Chichester. It was built hundreds of years ago for a rich merchant and his wife.'

'Who cares when it was built?' muttered Zoe. 'Someone put a log on that fire. It's freezing in here.'

A small fire was barely alight in the massive open fireplace. Zoe threw on another two logs and started blowing at the flames. Soon there was a lovely warm glow spreading through the entrance hall. The snow was settling now on the icy surface of the water. Ethan and Jacob took out their phones to let their parents know they were safe.

'Mine is completely dead,' said Jacob. 'I've tried to text my dad, but there seems to be no signal.'

'Me too,' said Ethan. 'I guess we'll have to wait for the storm to pass.'

*

Doc and the other fish watched helplessly as the Twolegs were rescued from the water and a thin layer of ice crept slowly across the golden lake. The water beneath the ice was still warm and clear. The goldfish were used to spending long sleepy weeks at the bottom of their ponds during the winter months. The cold water at this time of year usually made them drowsy, and even swimming would become very tiring. But this warm water didn't make them feel sleepy at all. If anything, it seemed to be full of energy and almost alive as they swam through it.

'The other creatures in town won't be able to venture out in this storm,' said Doc to his pals from the pond. 'This water doesn't feel right. We need to understand where it's coming from. Sharky, you swim along South Street down to the canal basin and see what you can find. Zorro and Fantail, you swim up North Street as far as you can. Ghost and Silver, come with me. We'll explore East Street. Let's meet back at the Cross.'

The spiders and the two mice that had brought them the news from the university were sheltering from the strange blizzard that now swept through the city.

They'd never seen a storm like it before. Great drifts of white snow covered the golden lake that had drenched their homes. Most of the city had lost power. Button and Stitchley watched as candles flickered in the windows of the houses along North Street.

Jacob's dad was also trapped out at the hospital. The advice was not to use the roads in these dreadful conditions and there were still plenty of patients there that needed his help. He was concerned that Jacob had not picked up any of his texts but guessed he was with his friends. He'd be fine.

Jacob soon got bored of looking out through the huge windows of Edes House at the swirling snow and wandered off to explore the rest of the building. Most of the grand rooms were now used for weddings. One of them was already prepared with rows of seats decorated with ribbons and silk flowers.

He strolled up the spiral staircase into a smaller room that was laid out for a business meeting of some kind. There was a large flip chart on an easel, and tables were arranged in a horseshoe shape so that everyone could see what was written on the chart. Jacob helped himself to a glass of water and a chocolate biscuit from a table laid out with pots of coffee and tea. He put a few biscuits in his pocket for his friends downstairs and wandered over to the flip chart at the front of the room. He whipped back the coversheet.

The first page had TOP SECRET written in large red letters. Underneath this, he could just about make out the words Project Chichester. Jacob couldn't resist it. He flipped over to the next page.

'Can I help you, young man?' whispered a creaky voice in his ear. Jacob swung around in surprise and saw Professor MacKrell's face inches from his own.

8 TRAPPED IN THE ATTIC.

By early evening, the snow was up to the roofs of the vehicles parked in the hospital car park. The golden waters might have stopped at the city wall, but the massive storm with all its snow covered the entire countryside. Jacob's dad was still stuck at the hospital; he was now very worried that he'd not heard from his son since he'd paddled across the lake in his canoe hours ago. The freak blizzard covered a large part of the

South Coast and was the lead news story on all the TV channels.

The reporters said that the snowstorm seemed to have started over the city of Chichester. It had spread out as far as Brighton in the east and Portsmouth in the west. Some scientists were blaming the Russians for creating some kind of weather bomb. Others were showing maps of fault lines in the earth's crust that might explain the rising waters and strange weather. All radio and mobile phone signals had been lost and most landlines were down.

The prime minister had declared a national emergency and ordered the army to send troops to the area. Some had already been helicoptered in and were setting up a base camp on the university playing fields. The temperature had dropped well below freezing and the soldiers urged everyone to stay indoors.

Doc and the other goldfish weren't cold at all. They were basking in the warm waters underneath the ice. They'd met back at the Cross after searching the lake for clues. Zorro and Fantail had made an interesting discovery at the top of North Street.

'As we reached the very edge of the lake, we noticed the current got stronger. It was as if we were swimming up rapids. We couldn't believe what we saw. There were two huge underground pipes feeding the lake with warm water.'

'We found the same sort of pipes at the end of East Street,' said Ghost and Silver, their shimmering white scales almost glowing in the sparkling water.

Sharky added, 'Have you noticed that it's still light down here, even though the surface is completely covered over? It's as if the water creates light as well as heat. I've never seen anything like it. I'm so pumped up. I feel I could swim to the end of the world.'

'This new freedom is wonderful for us,' replied Doc. 'We're no longer trapped in our pond and I can't deny that I love it, but it's not great for the land animals, least of all the Twolegs. We have no idea what's happening above our heads. Down here it's warm and exciting, but up there it could be very different.'

Up above was indeed very different, especially in Edes House. Professor MacKrell grabbed Jacob by the arm as other lecturers from the university rushed into the room, holding Zoe and Ethan. Zoe kicked and screamed until a chubby, balding teacher placed a cloth soaked in a liquid over her mouth that made her go limp.

'What have you done to her?' screamed Ethan.

'Calm down, sonny,' hissed the shiny-headed professor. 'It's just some chloroform. She'll be fine.'

The children were bundled up the staircase to a small attic room. The door slammed shut and they heard a key turn in the lock. Zoe was slumped against the wall. She was halfawake and muttering to herself. She used a lot of words that Jacob's dad would not be happy with and several that Jacob had never heard of before. He was fairly sure that she was not wishing their captors a Happy New Year and good health for the rest of their lives. The boys sat with her until she was well enough to nibble on one of the biscuits that Jacob had slipped into his pockets.

Ethan checked the walls for any secret doors, but there were none. Jacob sat quietly in a corner, trying to figure out what the heck had just happened. How had the professors escaped from the freezer and what did they have to do with the singing plants and freaky weather?

In the meeting room below them, Professor MacKrell was addressing a dozen or so of the other lecturers. He looked in perfect health with no signs of frostbite at all. He still wore his flowing black gown. He'd even found his old-fashioned mortar board, which balanced on his head at a precarious angle. His bulging grey eyes peered over the top of his gold-rimmed glasses.

'Our plan is nearly complete. We have taken the city,' he roared to much applause from the others seated at the tables around him. 'The fools fell for the simple magic trick of swapping our bodies for ice statues when the lights went out. Have they never been to a magic show? And to see those stupid kids putting them in the freezer. It was hysterical.'

There was more clapping and thumping of hands on the tables, which Professor MacKrell soaked up like an ageing actor waiting for a lifetime achievement award. He waited for the applause to die down and then continued.

'I'd like to thank Professor Skwidly for her ground-breaking work on storm creation. Surely worthy of a Nobel Prize, as are the years of dedication Professor Coddington has spent on mind control. The gases released from those rockets on New Year's Eve filled their heads with all sorts of rubbish. They really did think the plants were making music. Idiots, all of them! It has taken us decades to dig the tunnels from the university to carry the life-giving waters into the city. Professor Hakeman has worked for years on perfecting the formula that will create a new and exciting life for everyone.'

The room erupted into even louder cheers when Professor Coddington added, 'Well, for us fish anyway!'

9 MAGIC MIRRORS.

Jacob's father was desperate to leave the hospital, but the soldiers refused to let him go outside until the blizzard had weakened. He'd texted his son many times and heard nothing. He knew Jacob was a bright lad, but he'd give anything to be with him right now. Reports said that the weather was supposed to be better in the morning, so there was nothing to do but sit tight and wait.

The spiders, Button and

Stitchley, were also going nowhere. They were still shivering in a corner of their web in North Street. The mice from the university were fast asleep under a pile of jumpers yet to be sorted out for the charity shop. The dash across the park had been exhausting.

'There's nothing the creatures of Chichester can do until this storm passes,' said Button, shivering so hard that the whole web vibrated. But he was wrong.

In the warm waters beneath the snow, Doc had come up with a plan. The shoal of goldfish had been arguing for an hour or so. Ghost and Silver said they liked this new freedom to go anywhere and to escape from their small pond. They didn't feel the slightest bit hungry, even though they'd not eaten all day. They loved this new watery city.

Zorro and Sharky argued that, although it was fun to swim through the streets that they'd only ever heard dragonflies talk about, it was not really their home. It belonged to someone else: the creatures who breathed air.

Doc was also hugely excited to be out of his tiny pond but agreed with the darker goldfish that, at the end of the day, this was not where they were meant to be. They had to stop the flow of water.

Zorro said, 'Either side of the huge underground pipes in North Street were two large covers. They looked like massive dustbin lids that had been slid aside to allow the water to flood the city. Perhaps there was a way of sliding them back into place?'

'Don't be ridiculous. If they're enormous, we won't be able to move them, you idiot,' scoffed Sharky and flipped Zorro with his tail like someone might nudge a friend in the shoulder.

Zorro shot across the lake so fast that he was just a golden blur flashing past their eyes. He tumbled over and over in the golden waters, narrowly missing the Cross. He gulped water through his gills and found himself halfway to the cathedral before he knew it.

'I hardly touched him,' said a horrified Sharky. 'It was just a flick of my tail.'

The other fish swam over to Zorro to check that he was okay. They were there in a blink of an eye with just a few flaps of their fins.

'Wow. That was a bit freaky,' said Ghost. 'I know we said how full of energy we feel, but I think I've suddenly become Superfish. In fact, we all have!'

'Do you think we can fly?' asked Silver, eyes bright with excitement. 'Or move mountains?'

'I have no idea,' said Doc 'but I do know that those giant dustbin lids should be easy enough for us to move back in place whenever we want to.'

*

The young Twolegs in the attic of Edes House wished that they had super strength. Zoe had been kicking the door for the last five minutes, but it didn't budge. Ethan was still looking for a secret escape ladder or hidden door behind a bookcase, but had no luck. Then Jacob had an idea.

'We don't need to escape at all,' he said. The others stared at him as if he'd lost all hope and he just wanted to freeze to death in the cold dark room. 'We just have to make them think we've escaped. They're bound to come to check on us soon or bring us some food. We need to disappear.'

'What are you going to do,' asked Zoe, 'wave your magic wand and shout vanisheramus so we melt into the floor?'

'Something like that,' replied Jacob and explained what they had to do. 'Ethan, when you were searching for a hidden ladder did you look behind the huge mirrors leaning against the wall?'

'Yes, it was the first place I

looked. They're huge. I thought they might be hiding something.'

'Well, that's my plan. They will be hiding something – us!'

Zoe took off her boot to rub her bruised toe. 'Go on.'

'I saw this programme on the TV where a magician in Las Vegas made an elephant disappear in front of a crowd of thousands. But it was not real magic. He'd used mirrors to make it look like the room was empty. The elephant was right where he'd always been, hidden behind the mirrors. We need to do the same.'

The three friends moved the first mirror about two metres from the door of the attic. It was bigger than the whiteboard their teacher used at school and very heavy. They placed a second mirror that was just as large in position so it made a corner. After resting for a few seconds, they dragged a third mirror to the other side so that all three made a large U shape facing the door.

There were old desks and bookcases pushed up against the walls. They managed to drag these behind the mirrors to hold them in place. Muscles strained to move the heavy objects and at times they thought they'd have to give up. But they gritted their teeth and pushed with all their might until the job was done.

Zoe staggered in front of the mirrors and caught her breath. She did her pop-star pose and smiled at her reflections in all directions. If she wasn't so tired, she'd have done a little dance. When she peeped around the side of the mirrors, she was delighted that they reflected just the empty floor, walls, and ceiling.

'Won't they think it's strange that everything has gone, not just us?'

'I'm not sure it matters,' replied Jacob. 'We just need them to open the door so we can make a dash for it. Come on, let's hide behind the side mirror. I think I've left just enough space for us to push through. If there's more than one lecturer, make sure you wait until they are all in the room. If we break our cover too soon, there could be others waiting for us outside.'

'Then what's the plan?' asked Ethan. But before Jacob could answer, they heard footsteps on the stairs.

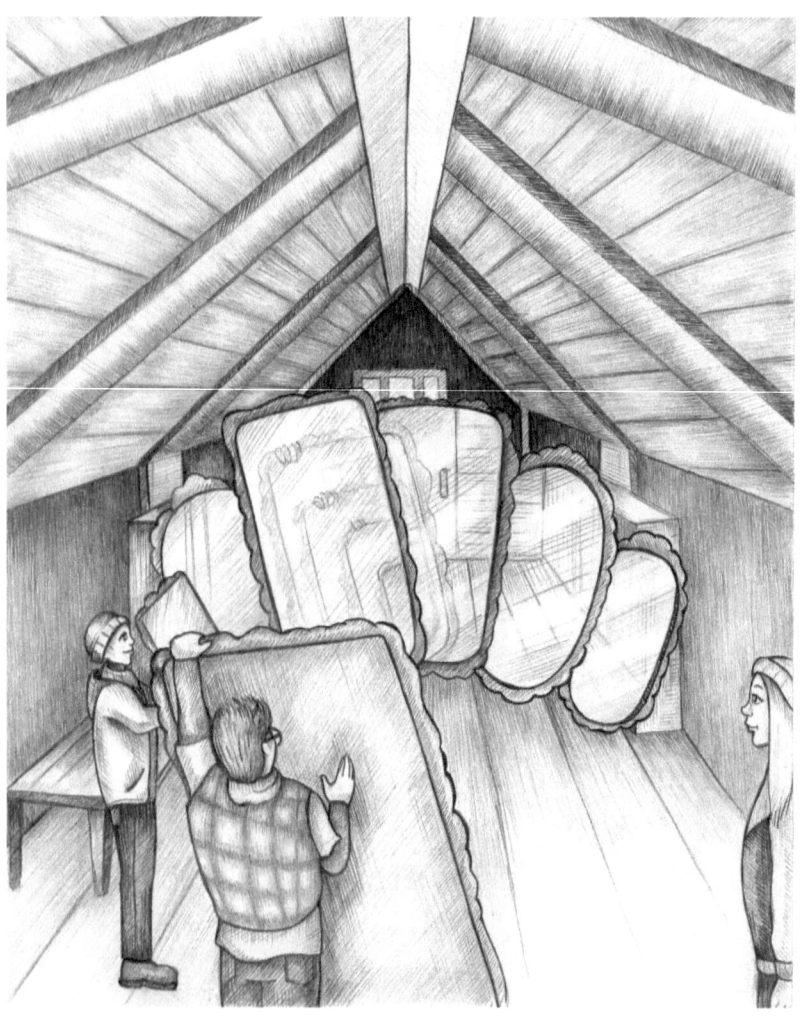

10 DASTARDLY PLANS REVEALED.

Zoe's heart was beating so loudly she was sure that it echoed around the room. Ethan bit his lip until it hurt; Jacob held his breath as they heard keys in the lock. The door was opened only a few inches as Professor MacKrell slid three food trays through the gap. As the door began to shut, he took just the briefest of looks into the room.

From where Jacob was hiding, he could see the smug look on

MacKrell's face change to one of shock. His huge eyes grew even bigger as he pushed his glasses farther up his nose.

'This can't be possible,' he shouted to what looked like an empty room as he shoved the door wide open and raced inside, tripping in his panic and falling flat on his face.

This was their chance. Zoe was the first out, making sure she stamped on MacKrell's glasses that had slid across the floor. Ethan jumped over the cloaked figure; Jacob was halfway out when he was grabbed by one ankle.

'You're not going anywhere,' hissed the lecturer as he searched for his specs with the other hand. Jacob kicked and twisted his foot, but the hand gripped tighter. He shouted to his friends, who were already on their way back up the stairs to help him. They grabbed his outstretched hands and tugged with all their might. There was a faint plopping sound as Jacob's boot slid off his foot. The red-faced professor tumbled back onto the floor.

He slammed into the back mirror that had been carefully balanced against the bookcases. It crashed to the floor in a thousand splinters of glass. The two side mirrors then wobbled a little before they too toppled into the room right on top of the writhing body of Professor MacKrell. They landed with a heavy thud but did not shatter. The room fell silent.

The body under the mirrors was almost completely hidden from view; just one hand could be seen holding on to Jacob's boot. Zoe bent down and wriggled it free.

'There's something very fishy going on here. Come on, Jacob, get your boot on; let's get out of this house. It gives me the creeps.'

The three friends crept down the spiral staircase in silence. Nobody in the rooms below them had heard the chaos in the attic. There seemed to be some sort of party going on with clapping and cheering.

'Make a break for the door and get help,' whispered Jacob to his friends. 'I need to see what's written on that flip chart.'

Ethan grabbed him by the shoulder. 'You can't be serious? It's too dangerous. Come on, let's go.' But Jacob was already on his way down the stairs to the meeting room. The cheering had stopped and someone was speaking. Zoe rolled her eyes and held one finger to her lips as they reluctantly followed Jacob down the staircase.

The door was wide open; Professor Coddington was at the flip chart.

'This is the plan to develop our work to the next stage,' he said, rolling back the page that said Top Secret. 'But let's leave that until after lunch. Professor Skwidly has prepared a fabulous buffet for us next door.

Let's take a break and come back to it once Professor MacKrell has dealt with those troublesome kids. There was so much poison in the food we left for them, I'm sure they are already dumped outside with the rest of the rubbish by now.'

The room cheered once more as they followed the scaly skinned professor through the doors to the next room to stuff their faces. The sliding doors between the two rooms were slid shut and the school pals crept in. Zoe stared at the flip chart but could not make head nor tail of it. It was written in some sort of code. Ethan slid his hand over the page.

'I've never seen anything like this before. It just doesn't make sense. The words are all jumbled up and letters seem to move around and float in space. It makes me dizzy just to look at it.'

Jacob also reached out to touch the paper. For the first time in his life everything written on the page was clear.

Each letter appeared bright and bold to him. The words sat heavily on the paper, as if they were waiting for him to read them out loud. To the others' utter amazement, he turned to the next page, muttering to himself, and then turned to the last page, understanding every word.

His friends had never seen him so calm and focused. They stepped away to leave him with his thoughts. Laughter erupted from the room next door, but Jacob hardly heard it. Ethan and Zoe held their breath as he flipped the chart back to the first page.

'This is bad. This is really bad,' he said. 'Chichester is just the start. We have to stop them before it's too late. Follow me. We need to get help.'

11 SUPERFISH TO THE RESCUE.

They tiptoed quietly out of the building onto the snow-covered steps of Edes House. Their canoes were still there, but useless on the frozen lake.

'We have no choice but to walk,' said Jacob. 'But first we need to get some warmer clothes. When I left the house this morning, it was cold, but not this cold. I noticed some scarfs hanging up in the cloakroom of the house. You wait here. I'll get them.'

Before the others could say a word, Jacob was heading back into the house. He disappeared for what seemed ages when Zoe noticed the curtains twitch in the meeting room above. A goggle-eyed professor peeped out at the storm, then down towards the steps. He leaned forward and pointed at Ethan and Zoe huddled together in the snow. In a single voice, they both shouted, 'JACOB, THEY'RE COMING.'

Jacob was still nowhere to be seen. Then the door flew open wide as he came hurtling out of the house with an arm full of scarfs, hats, and gloves.

'Run!' he yelled to the others as he sprinted past them.

They didn't stop to check if anyone was following until they were well past the old Cross in the centre of town. Finally, they paused for breath outside a fancy chocolate shop in East Street. Zoe was wondering if anyone would really mind if she smashed the window to grab a handful of mouth-watering, creamy chocolates when Jacob said,

'I saw their plans. You're not going to believe this, but those professors are not human at all. They are some sort of fish species living inside human bodies. They're testing their plan in Chichester, but then they aim to flood the whole of the UK. They want to build a massive wall that will keep the flood waters in and the rest of the world out.

But these floods will not just be a few metres deep. They're talking walls a hundred metres high.'

Ethan had a deep frown on his face. 'I don't mean to be unkind, Jacob, but are you feeling all right? Perhaps you banged your head when they threw you in the attic. I looked at that chart and it was all gobbledygook to me. Are you having a laugh? 'Cos it's not very funny.'

There was a mixed expression of anger and sadness on Jacob's face. Zoe put an arm on his shoulder. 'Hey, I believe you. What's your plan?'

'We need to get to the university and stop this snowstorm. It's all controlled from there.'

'I'm sorry, mate. It just seems so far-fetched,' said Ethan, looking down at his feet. 'But if you believe it, then that's good enough for me. Still friends?'

They gave each other a high five and trudged through the snow towards the university.

Huddled under the awning of that same chocolate shop was Beaky, the pigeon from the park. She'd heard every word and, although none of it made much sense to her, she knew she had to tell the spiders in North Street.

Button was still deep in thought at the centre of his web when he opened one of his eight eyes to see a cold and confused pigeon tapping at the window.

'It's Beaky,' said Stitchley as she crawled from her web towards the glass to hear what the bird was spinking.

'Three young Twolegs is going

to stop da fish at the university,' Beaky spinked as loudly as she could. 'Da fish are making it snow. Oh – and dey is building a wall, a really big one. It's going to go around everyfink.'

'Poor thing,' whispered Stitchley to her brother. 'I think she's lost her mind.'

'No, this is beginning to make sense,' said Button. 'The blizzard started in Chichester and I'm sure the flood is all part of some master plan. We need to gather as many creatures as we can that are able to cope in these awful conditions and get to the university.'

'I agree,' said Stitchley. 'Those young Twolegs may need our help. We creatures have done nothing so far but hide away.'

Stitchley was so very wrong. Doc, Zorro, and the other goldfish had already reached the huge pipes that were pumping water into the city at the top of North Street. The current was really strong, but with their new-found strength, they managed to swim towards the huge covers that had been slid aside to let the water flow. They arranged themselves along the side of one of the covers, and even though they pushed with all their might, nothing budged.

'We're just not strong enough,' said Zorro. 'This isn't going to work.'

Doc had already swum over to the cover on the other pipe. He swam to the very top and saw that there was a locking mechanism holding the massive metal plate in place. It was a large hook, like the end of a pirate's arm.

'We've got to release the hook first,' he said to the others. 'Come on, let's all get below it and push.'

The shoal of goldfish swam across the raging torrent of water and pushed hard, flapping their tails like mad. The hook popped up and they saw the circular door roll back to cover the pipe. They found a similar hook on the other cover and soon the gushing water was held back. The fish were delighted. They then swam at full speed to the pipes in East Street, where they quickly stopped the water flow there too.

'Well, I guess that's the end of our freedom,' said Sharky to the others. 'But, you know, I kind of miss my pond. I felt safe there and, although this has been an adventure I'll never forget, I think it's time to go home.'

The others nodded and followed Doc back towards their little pond in the centre of town. By the time they got back to Jacob's garden, the level of the water was already lower. They enjoyed their last few hours of freedom, exploring the garden before the water receded and they were safely back at home.

*

The journey to the university took the three children longer than they expected. The snow was knee deep towards the north of the city. When they finally reached the university, they saw the troops and helicopters.

'Wow,' gasped Ethan. 'It looks like they've sent half the army to help us.' He began to wave at the soldiers until Jacob grabbed his hand.

'Look, I'm sure you're right,' replied Jacob, 'but we don't know who to trust. Let's get inside and look around first.'

They entered University House and saw an amazing sight.

The Creatures of Chichester

12 ANIMAL ARMY ATTACK.

The main building at the university was two storeys high with curved steps leading up to a large door. Huge arched windows ran either side of the door, like the sort you see in an old church.

Above the door was a small spire sticking out from the grey sloping roof. The rest of the university was very modern with sports halls and artist studios, but University House was clearly quite old.

Inside the entrance of the building was a massive egg-shaped machine. It took up most of the space and was making a strange throbbing sound. The surface of the giant egg was glowing; the greenish light grew brighter in time with the throbbing noise. It looked alive.

Leading from the giant egg were dozens of cables that stretched up to the roof above. The friends were speechless. Then Ethan said, 'I think it's some sort of generator attached to the spire. I bet this is the storm maker.'

Zoe and Jacob remained silent. They just stared at the egg-shaped machine, drawn in by the throbbing sound. They didn't hear the footsteps behind them.

'We seem to have some visitors,' said a loud voice above the eerie noise of the machine.

They spun around and saw a tall man in white uniform; the sort that soldiers might wear at the North Pole. He had stars on the collar of his jacket and was probably a general or something like that. Four other soldiers stood just behind him, wearing dark glasses and holding machine guns.

'Thank goodness you're here,' said Zoe. There was a smile on her face for the first time in ages. 'You have to help us. They're going to drown everyone.' She raced over and hugged the general, which was the first time the boys had seen her hug anyone. Zoe was not the huggy type.

Jacob also stepped towards the first friendly face he'd seen all day. 'Sir, could you let me borrow your phone? We need to call our parents. My father is a doctor at the hospital. I need to let him know where I am.'

'No problem, young man. You all look frozen and hungry. Follow me and we'll get you some hot tea. Then you can tell us all about this flood of yours.'

He pushed Zoe away from his body as if he also was not used to being hugged by anyone. The soldiers behind him stood to attention. Ethan was about to protest that they had no time to lose, but he was rather cold and a cup of hot tea sounded wonderful. He nodded his agreement and they followed the soldiers along a corridor, feeling safe for the first time all day. The general opened the door of a small room and smiled at Zoe. 'Ladies first.' He almost bowed as she entered the room, followed by the boys, who were not so impressed.

The door slammed hard and they heard bolts slam into place.

'Send a message to Professor MacKrell at Edes House,' they heard the general bellow to his troops. 'And guard this door. These brats could spoil everything. We'll deal with them later.'

*

At the bottom of College Lane, the road leading up to the university, there was another small army gathering. But this one was not dressed in uniform. It was made up of about thirty dogs led by Knuckles, the street-wise dog from the butcher's, and twenty cats led by the magnificent Bengal cat, Purrcasso, from the art gallery. Perched in the trees were a squadron of pigeons led by Beaky, who had done a magnificent job in spreading the word amongst the creatures of Chichester.

The spiders, Button and Stitchley, had gathered the army together and were now safely tucked inside the warm fur of Knuckles as they crept slowly across the playing fields towards University House. Pesto was desperate to come along, but Laplancha said that the snow was just too deep, so they stayed at the charity shop, where Pesto sulked in a corner.

The animal army slid along the hedges so silently that the soldiers on duty never heard a thing. The birds had already reported that a weird egg-shaped machine could be seen in the building that was guarded by troops.

Knuckles led a charge up the steps beneath the feet of four soldiers who were about to enter the building. A deafening sound of barking startled the troops, who had little time to reach for their guns.

The dogs swarmed into the building, biting and snarling. They were quickly followed by an army of cats that scratched and bit at the soldiers' arms and faces. A few shots were fired, but soon the terrified Twolegs were fleeing for their lives. Pigeons dive-bombed them as they rushed across the garden, splattering their uniforms with a heavy dose of pigeon poo for good measure.

Knuckles saw the soldiers guarding the door to the room where the young Twolegs were shouting to be released. One of them threw open the door with the intention of taking one of the children hostage. Knuckles raced down the corridor towards him.

The soldier grabbed Zoe, but she stamped hard on his foot, twisted to face him, and delivered a well-aimed knee to his groin. He yelped in pain and hesitated for a moment, but saw that the other men were already well down the corridor. He dropped the young Twoleg as Knuckle's bit hard into his ankle.

The children were gobsmacked to see dozens of dogs and cats chasing away their captors, and at first were quite alarmed. Ethan, in particular, was not very keen on dogs. It soon became clear that they were only attacking the so-called soldiers.

'Let's get to the roof,' shouted Jacob above all the barking and hissing. They rushed up the stairs to where the cables from the egg-shaped machine were attached to the spire. With no thought for their own safety, they yanked away the cables; a small disc of blue sky appeared above their heads. It spread quickly, banishing the drifting snow. As suddenly as it had appeared, the blizzard ceased and even the air temperature felt warmer.

Ethan pointed to the helicopters taking off from the playing fields below them.

'Those cowards are retreating,' screamed Zoe at the top of her voice and did a little victory dance.

With the storm banished, there was a mass of bleeping and ringing as everyone's phones burst into life. Jacob looked at fifty missed calls from his dad. Tears ran down his face as he spoke to him for the first time in days and told him he was safe.

His friends were also sobbing as they rang their loved ones and tried to explain what had happened. They hardly noticed the dogs and cats slink away and of course never even caught sight of Button and Stitchley, who had masterminded the operation, clinging on for dear life under Knuckles' collar.

*

The following weeks were full of press interviews and appearances on TV. Jacob, Zoe, and Ethan became worldwide celebrities and even received a letter from the Queen. The helicopters had landed at Edes House to pick up their fish-eyed masters and disappeared over the horizon.

Some say they were whisked into space; others said they must have developed some sort of cloaking device so that they could not be tracked by radar. Either way, they were never seen again.

The ice eventually melted and the golden waters receded to just a few puddles left here and there. The two mice, Pesto and Laplancha, never returned to the university; they set up home with the spiders in North Street instead.

Button and Stitchley were glad that they'd helped clear the huge storm; sadly they had no idea about the major role played by Doc and his friends to stop the floods.
But the shoal of goldfish in Jacob's pond knew that just because they couldn't be heard, and were rarely seen, didn't mean they were invisible. Doc would make sure that the other creatures would not ignore them in the future.

And just because Jacob saw things in a different way to others, nobody would ever ignore him again either.

Christopher Joyce

ABOUT THE AUTHOR

Christopher Joyce is a Twoleg from Chichester in West Sussex, England. He has been a teacher, marketing director, waiter, once made Venetian blinds, worked in a steel works and has run a garden design business.

Also by Christopher Joyce

The Creatures of Chichester:
the one about the stolen dog

The Creatures of Chichester:
the one about the mystery blaze.

The Creatures of Chichester:
the one about the smelly ghosts.

The Creatures of Chichester:
the one about the curious cloud.

The Creatures of Chichester:
the one about the edible aliens.
Find out more at
www.creaturesofchichester.com

Christopher Joyce

www.ingramcontent.com/pod-product-compliance
Lightning Source LLC
Chambersburg PA
CBHW020618300426
44113CB00007B/698